Contents

Prologue: The Big Slide 1
1 Estoril, 2006 5
2 Beginnings 14
3 Bitter 28
Lap 1 47
4 A Teenage Dream 51
Lap 2 69
5 The Ravine 73
Lap 3 92
6 The Game 96
Lap 4 111
7 The King 116
Lap 5 136
8 Ring of Fire 141
Lap 6 159
9 The Pretenders 163
Lap 7 181
10 Endgame 185
Lap 8 203
11 WANTED! 207
Lap 9 218
12 The Wake-Up Call 222
Lap 10 239

13	Death and Taxes	244
Lap 11		260
14	Bad Blood	264
Lap 12		282
15	The Reckoning	286
Lap 13		303
16	Motegi, 2008	308
Last Lap		321
Epilogue: A Kind of Living		326
Index		331

RING OF FIRE

The Inside Story of Valentino Rossi and MotoGP

Rick Broadbent

BANTAM PRESS

LONDON • TORONTO • SYDNEY • AUCKLAND • JOHANNESBURG

TRANSWORLD PUBLISHERS
61–63 Uxbridge Road, London W5 5SA
A Random House Group Company
www.rbooks.co.uk

First published in Great Britain
in 2009 by Bantam Press
an imprint of Transworld Publishers

A CIP catalogue record for this book
is available from the British Library.

ISBN 9780593062630

Addresses for Random House Group Ltd companies outside the UK
can be found at: www.randomhouse.co.uk
The Random House Group Ltd Reg. No. 954009

The Random House Group Limited supports The Forest Stewardship Council (FSC), the leading international forest-certification organization. All our titles that are printed on Greenpeace-approved FSC-certified paper carry the FSC logo. Our paper procurement policy can be found at
www.rbooks.co.uk/environment

Typeset in 11/16pt Berling by
Falcon Oast Graphic Art Ltd.
Printed and bound in Great Britain by
Clays Ltd, Bungay, Suffolk

2 4 6 8 10 9 7 5 3 1

FSC
Mixed Sources
Product group from well-managed
forests and other controlled sources
www.fsc.org Cert no. TT-COC-2139
© 1996 Forest Stewardship Council